Writing Toward JUSTICE

The Life and Reporting of
ALICE A. DUNNIGAN

Peggy Thomas

Illustrated by
Tonya Engel

CALKINS CREEK

AN IMPRINT OF ASTRA BOOKS FOR YOUNG READERS
New York

Growing up in Russellville, Kentucky, Alice knew all about injustice. It lingered in the red clay her father farmed, in the white people's clothes her mother washed, and in the stories of enslavement her grandparents told.

But Alice ached to tell different stories.
Stories of . . .

...SPIRIT.

At four, Alice longed to go to school.

    Mother said she was too young.

    Father said a sharecropper's daughter didn't need an education.

    Little Alice marched off on her own.

    But girls mocked her straighter hair and lighter skin. Ashamed, Alice fell silent.

    Until she found another way to speak out.

"You stay out of that place!" Mother warned.
   But it wasn't fair!
   Alice had to *go*!
   Head high, she marched inside.
   From that day on, Alice fought injustice wherever she found it.

No one heard of Alice's restroom rebellion. The town newspaper only printed white people's news.

How could anyone care about something they didn't know was going on?

Alice dashed off a letter to the nearest Black-owned paper and asked for a job.

Would they take a chance on a thirteen-year-old?

Alice loved reporting. There was just one problem. The *Owensboro Enterprise* couldn't afford to pay her. So, Alice sold newspapers. The more people she named in her stories, the more papers she sold.

Soon, she made the news, too.

Alice became the family's first high school graduate!
First college grad would come next.

Working her way through school
lugging dirty dishes and washing
people's laundry left little room for
writing. And when she graduated, the
only job she could get was teaching in a
one-room schoolhouse.

MARY E. MERRITT

GENERAL CHARLES YOUNG

NELLIE CONLEY

DR. MARY ELLEN BRITTON

Alice loved teaching, but one thing troubled her. How was she supposed to teach history when there were no Black heroes in the history books?

Alice took up her pen. She wrote short biographies of famous Kentuckians for her students. She also sent them to the local paper. More people needed to know their history, especially at a time when a dark cloud loomed over the nation.

EFFIE WALLER SMITH

AC MURPHY

OLIVER LEWIS

WOODSON

HERITAGE

Banks closed. People lost their jobs. Alice's pay was cut in half! She'd need a second job besides teaching.

   Fortunately, the government created a work program.
   Unfortunately, no one of color was hired.
   Alice marched down to the office and demanded fairness.
   But once hired, she found herself kneeling in the cemetery washing tombstones!
   Luckily, that job didn't last long.

The editor of the *Louisville Leader* had read Alice's biographies. He offered her a job.

OPPORTUNITY

Alice learned to proofread.
Compose headlines. AND she
had her own column about
Black women in American
history.

Still, Alice itched to write
a different kind of history.
History in the making.

But the world was at war.

America had just joined the Second World War. Millions of people enlisted or joined the workforce. One day, Alice saw a poster. TYPISTS NEEDED IN WASHINGTON DC.

Surely, history was happening there!

During the exam, Alice's nervous fingers skipped lines and doubled letters. But her essay was so good, officials let her retake the typing test.

This time, she took a deep breath and calmed her nerves.

FAITH

At night, Alice typed in a government office. During the day, she hunted for a reporting job.

Part time at first, Alice worked for the Associated Negro Press supplying stories to more than one hundred Black papers across the country. The pay was pitiful, yet Alice loved it.

Most of it.
In white neighborhoods, cabbies refused
to pick her up. Doormen shut her out. It was as if a giant
WHITES ONLY sign hung over much of the city! To get the story . . .
Alice hiked across town.
And marched past doormen.
She shared other people's struggles, too.
Struggles of crowded classrooms.
Of Black veterans kicked off busses.
Of voters arrested at the ballot box.
But Alice knew nothing would ever change unless people also heard stories of . . .

...COURAGE.

So, Alice sat beside protestors.
   Marched along picket lines.
   Comforted mourning families.
   Each story rippled across the country,
sparking more activism.
   Was the government paying attention?
   Alice marched into the Capitol to find out.

"Excuse me, Ma'am," a guard said. "You're not allowed inside without a press pass."

But they were only given to *white* reporters!

Alice vowed to get a press pass. She filled out the application and waited.

For weeks! But Alice did not give up.

Finally, the Senate held a hearing.

EQUALITY

ALICE A. DUNNIGAN BECOMES THE FIRST BLACK WOMAN REPORTER ADMITTED TO THE CAPITOL PRESS CORPS!

TRUTH

Alice clenched her fists and gritted her teeth as congressmen spewed racial insults. Some laughed at equal rights for workers. Others threatened the right to vote.

Alice would not let them get away with it!

And she'd keep an eye on other parts of government, too. She applied to and became the first Black woman reporter in the State Department.

The Supreme Court.

The White House!

So many questions swirled in Alice's head. She'd heard that President Harry S. Truman supported civil rights. But would he fight for Black veterans? How would he protect voting rights?

Unfortunately, Alice could barely see the president let alone ask a question.

Fortunately, Truman was planning a cross-country train
trip and reporters were welcome if they paid their way.
   Alice scrimped on food.
   Mended old clothes.
   And pawned her watch.

Onboard, there were flowers from Mrs. Truman. Fruit baskets from local farmers. Alice was beginning to feel part of the team.

But in Cheyenne, Wyoming, a soldier grabbed Alice's arm! "Get back behind the ropes!" he growled.

Alice held her ground.
Another reporter ran to Alice's rescue. Only then did the soldier let her go.
Straightening her hat, Alice brushed off the fear. And marched on.

RECOGNITION

Later, President Truman heard about the scuffle. "If you have any further trouble," he said, "let me know."

Alice DID!

She let him know EVERYTHING that troubled her and the Black community.

When will you improve schools?

Will you guarantee equal pay?

How will you protect voters' rights?

Finally, people of all races began to pay attention.

The battle for civil rights was just beginning.
Countless people would struggle, and
Alice would give them voice.
There would be other presidents, and
she'd keep them accountable, too.
For the rest of her life, Alice A. Dunnigan
would continue to use her words as a
moving force, writing America toward . . .

JUSTICE.

"It is my fondest hope that the story of my life and work will . . . encourage more young writers to use their talents as a moving force . . . and that their efforts will soon result in giving Americans the kind of nation that those of my generation so long hoped and worked for."

AUTHOR'S NOTE

A book can never hold a person's entire life, and this is especially true for Alice A. Dunnigan who was more than just a groundbreaking journalist. Alice was one of the first female sports reporters. She was an innovative educator who taught Black history when no one else did. She was an activist who spoke out against racial injustice, and as the first Black woman appointed to a presidential committee, she was an advocate for equal employment opportunities. Alice was also a hardworking single parent. During her teaching career, Alice married and divorced twice. She had a son, Robert, with her second husband, Charles Dunnigan. Alice moved to Washington, DC, in part to support her son, who stayed in Russellville, Kentucky, with her parents.

As a journalist, Alice challenged people in power, asked the questions that white reporters refused to ask, and held politicians accountable. "Without black writers," she said, "the world would perhaps never have known of the chicanery, shenanigans, and buffoonery employed by those in high places to keep the black man in his (proverbial) place."

Alice A. Dunnigan: pioneering journalist, civil rights activist, educator, and author

But Alice's real superpower was the ability to see a brighter future. While she was chronicling the beginning of the civil rights movement she was also struggling for her own rights as an African American and a woman. Every door she opened for herself she fought to keep open for those who would come after. Her grandson once asked if she had ever been afraid, and Alice replied, "Fear is the underside of courage. The deeper your fear, the stronger your courage."

This book is for courageous children everywhere.

—Peggy Thomas

ALICE A. DUNNIGAN 1906–1983

1906 Born Alice Allison, April 27, in Russellville, Kentucky.

1919 Reports for the *Owensboro Enterprise* (KY) at the age of 13.

1924–1942 Teaches in segregated schools in Todd County, Kentucky.

1947 Becomes Washington Bureau chief for Associated Negro Press; admitted to Capitol, White House, and State Department press corps.

1948 Travels with President Truman.

1961 Joins presidential Committee on Equal Employment Opportunity.

1967 Serves on President Kennedy's Commission on Youth Opportunity.

1974 Publishes autobiography, *A Black Woman's Experience: From Schoolhouse to White House.*

1982 Publishes *The Fascinating Story of Black Kentuckians.*

1983 Dies May 6, at the age of 77, in Washington, DC.

2019 Installation of a 6-foot bronze statue of Alice, created by Amanda Matthews, at the SEEK (Struggles for Emancipation and Equality in Kentucky) Museum, in Russellville, Kentucky.

2022 Honored by the White House Correspondents' Association with the first-ever Dunnigan-Payne Prize for Lifetime Career Achievement.

NEWSWORTHY WOMEN

Alice was one of many amazing Black women in the history of journalism. Here are a few more.

Mary Ann Shadd Cary (1823–1893) First African American woman newspaper publisher in North America.

Ida B. Wells (1862–1931) News editor and investigative journalist who exposed segregation and lynching.

Marvel Jackson Cooke (1903–2000) First African American woman to report for a white-owned mainstream newspaper.

Ethel Payne (1911–1991) Although Alice broke ground for her at the White House, Ethel remained in news longer and became known as "First Lady of the Black Press."

Carole Simpson (1940–) First African American woman to anchor a major network news program.

Isabel Wilkerson (1961–) First African American woman to win a Pulitzer Prize in journalism.

Rashida Jones (1981–) First Black woman to be president of a major television news network.

Alice A. Dunnigan on the steps of the Capitol, 1947

BIBLIOGRAPHY

All quotations used in the book can be found in the following sources marked with an asterisk (*).

Atlanta Daily News. "Newswoman of 'Firsts' Tells of Pioneering." April 28, 1955.

Atlanta Daily World. "Hotel Jim Crows Reporters at D.C. Press Conference." December 20, 1947.

Baltimore Afro-American. "Pioneering No 'Bed of Roses,' Mrs. Dunnigan Tells Iotas." May 7, 1955.

Black Women Oral History Project. Interviews, 1976–1981. Alice Allison Dunnigan. OH-31. Schlesinger Library, Radcliffe Institute, Harvard University, Cambridge, MA.

Chicago Defender. "Set Hearing on Hiring Policy Rules; Alice Dunnigan Named Consultant." June 15, 1961.

Daily Defender (Chicago). "Racial Insults Ring Out in House Debate." July 19, 1956, daily edition.

*Dunnigan, Alice A. *A Black Woman's Experience: From Schoolhouse to White House*. Pittsburgh: Dorrance, 1974.

*———. *Alone atop the Hill: The Autobiography of Alice Dunnigan, Pioneer of the National Black Press*. Edited by Carol McCabe Booker. Athens: University of Georgia Press, 2015.

*Gregory, John. "Alice Allison Dunnigan - Pioneering Journalist." *Connections*. Kentucky Educational Television, October 27, 2019. ket.org/program/connections/alice-allison-dunnigan-pioneering-journalist-25286/.

Jackson, Leigh. "Alice Dunnigan: Blazing the Trail." *Washington Post*, February 8, 1990.